EXPLORE
ANCIENT
WORLDS

THE
CELTS
OF THE BRITISH ISLES

TAMMY GAGNE

Mitchell Lane
PUBLISHERS

P.O. Box 196
Hockessin, Delaware 19707
Visit us on the web: www.mitchelllane.com
Comments? email us: contactus@mitchelllane.com

Ancient Assyria • Ancient Athens
The Aztecs • Ancient Babylon
The Byzantine Empire • The Celts of the British Isles
Ancient China • Ancient Egypt
Ancient India/Maurya Empire • Ancient Sparta

Copyright © 2013 by Mitchell Lane Publishers

ABOUT THE AUTHOR: Tammy Gagne is the
author of numerous books for adults and
children, including *A Kid's Guide to the Voting
Process* and *My Guide to the Constitution:
The Power of the States* for Mitchell Lane
Publishers. She has always been fascinated by
Celtic culture, in part due to her own Scottish
heritage. She resides in northern New England
with her husband and son.

PUBLISHER'S NOTE: The facts on which the story
in this book is based have been thoroughly
researched. Documentation of such research
can be found on page 46. While every
possible effort has been made to ensure
accuracy, the publisher will not assume liability
for damages caused by inaccuracies in the
data, and makes no warranty on the accuracy
of the information contained herein.

Printing   1   2   3   4   5   6   7   8   9

**Library of Congress
Cataloging-in-Publication Data**
Gagne, Tammy.
 The Celts of the British Isles / by Tammy Gagne.
     p. cm.—(Explore ancient worlds)
 Includes bibliographical references and index.
 ISBN 978-1-61228-283-1 (library bound)
 1. Celts—Great Britain—Juvenile literature. 2.
Civilization, Celtic—Juvenile literature. I. Title.
 DA140.G33 2012
 941'.004916—dc23
                                        2012009414

eBook ISBN: 9781612283586

PLB

CONTENTS

A reconstruction of the tomb found in Hochdorf, Germany

An Exciting Discovery

Imagine the excitement of discovering an ancient burial ground. Being the first human to uncover a grave dating back more than 2,500 years would be a thrilling event. The only thing that might make it more exciting is finding numerous artifacts that tell stories about the ancient people buried within it. This is the kind of discovery that most archaeologists only dream about. For Dr. Jörg Biel, however, it really happened.

In 1978, a schoolteacher from Hochdorf, a small German village, suggested that Biel and his team should inspect several mounds near her village. At first he didn't find anything. Then he struck paydirt. Biel unearthed one of the oldest burial sites in all of Europe. It was also one of the best preserved. It appeared that no one else had been inside the tomb since its construction around 550 BCE. About 40 other graves from this time period had been found in various locations around Europe, but this one was different. Everything inside remained untouched by human hands since being placed there. Because it remained undisturbed since it was created, this tomb provided a great deal of information about an ancient group of people called the Celts.

The tomb was located deep inside a mound of earth about 200 feet (60 meters) wide and about 20 feet (6 meters) high. The mound was enclosed by a circle of stones. In the center of the mound was a hole that led to a wooden chamber. And inside that chamber was yet another chamber.

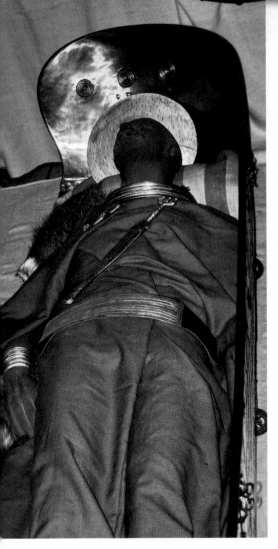

The bronze couch

Getting to these chambers was not an easy task. More than 50 tons of stones and oak logs had been placed around them to protect the tomb from intruders.

Inside the tomb Biel found the remains of a Celtic chieftain. He had been about 40 years old when he died. All that remained of his body was a skeleton, but it had much to tell the archaeologist and his team. The chieftain had been about six feet (1.85 meters), especially tall for that time. His body had been placed on a large bronze couch and adorned with gold, bronze, and amber. He had a neck ring made of sheet gold, a gold bracelet, and a belt with a gold plate in its center. Even the iron dagger that lay at his side was enclosed in a gold sheath. In all he wore more than 600 grams (21 ounces) of gold jewelry and other ornaments.[1]

Very little of the chieftain's clothing remained. The only piece the team could identify was a hat made from birch bark. It looked a lot like the hat on a sandstone figure of a man found at a nearby site. The team suspected that the hat was a special one worn only by Celts of great power. The man's head rested on the remains of a pillow made from braided grass, and underneath him were cushions made from wall hangings and animal furs. He was obviously a very important person.

In addition to the body and ornaments, the tomb also contained a four-wheeled wagon. On it rested nine bronze plates, three basins, and an axe. Nine drinking horns that matched the plates hung from the tomb's south

Gilded in preparation for the afterlife, this 42 centimeter long, bronze and iron dagger was carried by the chieftain in life. The blade was protected by a richly decorated sheath. The gold coating made for the burial consisted of 16 parts, all precisely fitted onto the dagger without any fold.

rf princely burial

rt DE
30 BC

r

al objects were
preparation
terlife.

er, which the
ied in life, was
onze and iron;
vas protected
decorated

ating made
l consisted

recisely
e dagger

wall. What did all this mean? The archaeologists were unsure. The wagon might have been used as a hearse when the chieftain died. Another possibility is that it had been buried in the tomb to carry him to a place the Celts called the Otherworld. Some versions of the Otherworld said it would be similar to the Christian heaven, with eternal youth, perfect weather, the chance to hunt, enjoy feasts and other pleasurable activities. In others, it was dark and gloomy, filled with monsters and other horrors. Still others believed that people who died would later be reborn after spending a period of time in the Otherworld.

The wagon found in the Hochdorf tomb can now be seen in a nearby museum.

The cauldron

Some of the artifacts in the tomb were from other parts of the world. A cauldron, for example, came from Italy. The presence of these items told the archaeologists that the Celts were traders. The number of plates and drinking horns – exactly nine – told the team other things about Celtic culture. This number nine was an important one in Greek culture. It was the ideal number for a symposium, a Greek drinking party. Finding these items suggested that the Celtic chieftain enjoyed feasting with friends. It also told the team that the chieftain and his people had been familiar with Greek traditions.

Biel and his team learned much about the Celts from studying the contents of the tomb at Hochdorf. Today, the era in which this tomb was constructed is a part of what is called the Hallstatt Period. This is because the first artifacts from this period were found in an Austrian village called Hallstatt. The Hallstatt Period spanned more than 300 years, from about

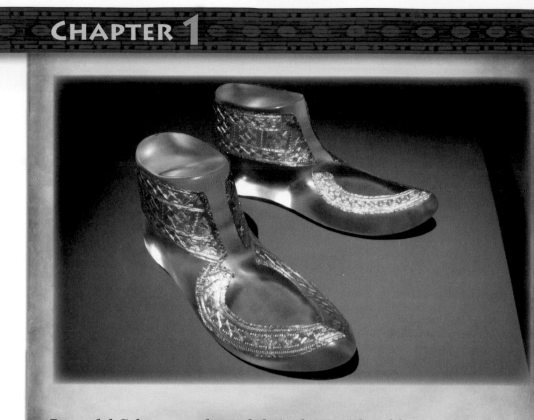

Powerful Celts even adorned their shoes with gold.

800 to 450 BCE. This era is thought to be the beginning of the Celtic culture.

The Celts were one of the largest groups of people who ever lived in Europe. Their culture covered a vast area, from the British Isles and Spain in the west to Asia Minor (the area we now call Turkey) in the east. Because they were never united under a single leader, it can be hard to understand exactly what made a Celt a Celt. The Celtic people did not even use this exact name. The Greeks call the Celts Keltoi. The Greeks may have come up with this term, or they may have based it on a word the Celts used for themselves. Whatever they called themselves, the Celts belonged to numerous separate yet similar clans that shared a common history, language, and basic religion.[2]

Salt of the Ancient Earth

In ancient societies salt was in many ways more valuable than gold. Many people might think of salt as unhealthy, since today we are constantly reminded that too much salt is a bad thing for our health. Yet the human body needs a certain amount of salt in order to function. Before the

Inside a salt mine

invention of appliances like freezers and refrigerators, salt was also used to preserve food. Without it, people had no way of keeping food fresh for long periods of time.

Spilling salt was thought to be bad luck. Many ancient people believed that a demon often nudged the hands of those who spilled salt. This is how the practice of throwing a pinch of salt over one's shoulder arose. The act was thought to ward off the demon.[3]

Archaeologists have discovered that salt mining was an important part of Celtic life during the Hallstatt Period. It isn't surprising that the people who owned the land where these mines were found were among the wealthiest of all Celts. There even seems to have been a Celtic class system based on the salt mines. The rich owned and oversaw the mines, and the poor worked in them.

Shafts more than 350 feet deep with wooden shovels and leather sacks still inside them have been found. Wooden tools were used for mining, because salt destroyed iron. Ancient miners used these tools to bring rock salt from inside the mines to the surface where the salt itself could then be extracted.

The Kleinaspergle,
a Celtic grave mound near Asperg, Germany

The Development of the Ancient Celts

In 1879, about a century before Biel discovered Hochdorf, German archaeologist Oscar Fraas began digging into a hill in western Germany called the Kleinaspergle. For centuries local farmers had noticed that this hill was different from the others around it. Natural hills are oddly shaped and rocky. The Kleinaspergle, however, was strangely smooth and round. This hill also stood alone, whereas most hills are part of chains of rising and falling terrain.

Fraas had previously discovered other tumuli, or mounds of earth, that had been created as burial sites. He suspected that this hill had also been created for this purpose. It wasn't unusual for ancient people to pile earth on top of gravesites the way we place tombstones over them today.

It also wasn't unusual for these burial sites to contain valuable items such as gold and jewels. Fraas uncovered two large stone chambers. He soon found out that he wasn't the first to search this particular tumulus for treasure, as the first one was empty. Luckily, he continued digging until he got to the inner chamber. It contained numerous artifacts from a Celtic period called La Tène, which arose immediately after the Hallstatt period.

Among the items were bronze sculptures, drinking horns, and Greek cups called kylikes. These items helped Fraas figure out when the tomb was created. Kylikes had already been dated to approximately 450 BCE. This told Fraas that the Kleinaspergle could be no older than this.

Celtic Britain and Northern Gaul
1st Century B.C.

Around 500 BCE the group of Celts called La Tène was developing in Switzerland. This group was named after a shallow spot in Lake Neuchâtel, near where the group had lived. La Tène is French for "the shallow place."[1]

La Tène Celts are known for both their art and their technology. They appear to have been the first Celts to use spiral patterns on their pottery, metal ornaments, and weapons. These designs later became very popular among all Celts. Knives, spearheads, and swords are among the most common artifacts that have been found from this period. These discoveries tell us that La Tène culture focused greatly on making and using weaponry.

Archaeologists break La Tène culture down into several shorter smaller periods. According to one version, La Tène A, the start of La Tène culture, marks the time between 450 and 390 BCE. Most artifacts from this time bear the spiral patterns for which the group is known.

La Tène B refers to the years between 390 and 300 BCE. During this time, many Celts migrated across Europe. As they moved around, they shared La Tène culture with new people. In turn the new people shared their cultures with the Celts. The result was a mixture of traditional Celtic art and artistic styles from the other groups. It can be difficult to identify items from this period, because they are often so different from each other. The one thing they do have in common is that so many of them are weapons. The Celts of this time valued their weapons greatly and had a reputation for being excellent and fearsome warriors.

La Tène C, which occurred from 300 to 75 BCE, was a lot like La Tène B. The biggest difference was that La Tène C included the minting of silver coins. The Celts created their coins themselves, but the artifacts are very similar to Greek and Roman coins. This tells us that Mediterranean civilizations were beginning to influence Celtic culture during this time.

La Tène technology focused on the use of iron. The Celts combined their tools with trade to increase the types and amount of food they could grow. These changes increased their population, which made it necessary for the Celts to acquire more land. The Celts expanded into different areas of Europe, often fighting for the land.

La Tène D marks the years between 75 and 10 BCE. This period marks major changes in Celtic culture. More coins are found from this time. The number of weapons made during this time, however, decreased from La Tène C. Instead the Celts were making more hand tools and farm equipment. This change was likely due to the size and power of the Roman military, which began expanding into their lands. The Celts knew they could not beat the Romans. As a result they were becoming less warlike.

The Celts had never been as united as the Romans. The Romans were part of one large group that acted together. The Celts belonged to different clans, each with its own chieftain. These chieftains often fought with one another. This made it difficult for the Celts to become powerful. The Romans and Greeks saw them as fearless to the point of being foolish.

This painting shows Gallic chieftain Vercingetorix (on horse) surrendering to Roman leader Julius Caesar (in red) at the Battle of Alesia

Though the Romans were more powerful than the Celts, this does not mean that Celtic culture came to an end. The Celts were very proud of their way of life. They may have stopped expanding into new lands, but they continued to develop in terms of their art, farming, and trading. Their language and religion also survived the end of their expansion eastward. Even to this day signs of Celtic influence can be found throughout Europe.

Celtic language can be divided into two dialects: Continental and Insular. The Continental Celtic dialect was spoken throughout Europe. The Insular Celtic dialect was spoken specifically in Great Britain, Ireland, and Brittany.[2] Although neither is spoken today, both dialects had an effect on modern languages on the continent. Welsh, Gaelic, and even modern English all include traces of Celtic words. For example, the names of the cities of Lyon, France, and London, England, come from the Celtic name Lugh, which was the name of the Celtic sun god.[3]

Tools of Ancient History

Archaeologists often divide history before the modern era into three ages, according to the level of technology: Stone Age, Bronze Age, and Iron Age. The Stone Age began more than two million years ago. During this time, most tools and weapons were made from stone. People sharpened stones to make hand axes, awls, spears, and knives.

Celtic bronze axe heads

The Bronze Age began around 3300 BCE. In this period, people learned to combine metals like copper, lead, and tin to make bronze. This new material was virtually indestructible. Weapons made from bronze were deadly. Bronze was certainly strong, but it was also extremely heavy. It could be difficult to find the materials needed to make bronze. Copper and tin were both plentiful resources, but often they were not found in the same area.

The Iron Age began around 1200 BCE and brought even better tools. Like bronze, iron was strong, but iron weighed slightly less. Iron could also take a sharper edge, which made both tools and weapons made from this metal even more efficient. Additionally, iron could be sharpened, whereas bronze could not. If a bronze tool or weapon became dull, it needed to be melted and re-cast. The rise of the Celts began during the Bronze Age, but they quickly moved into the Iron Age along with the rest of Europe.

The holiday Imbolc marked the beginning of lambing season.

Celtic Beliefs

The Celts had four main festivals that revolved around the seasons which were important to farmers. Starting on the evening of October 31—when today we dress up in costumes for Halloween—and continuing into the morning of November 1, the Celts celebrated Samhain. It marked the beginning of the Celtic New Year. It marked the end of the year's harvest and the beginning of winter. This ancient holiday actually has quite a bit in common with modern-day Halloween. The Celts believed that on this one day of the year, spirits from the Otherworld could move freely into the world of the living and vice versa. Over time this event evolved into the Christian holiday of All Saints Day.

In modern times, February 2 is known as Groundhog Day. In the time of the ancient Celts, this day was known as Imbolc. Like Samhain, Imbolc was celebrated by the Celts beginning on the previous evening. Instead of being about the dead, however, Imbolc was very much about the living. It marked the beginning of spring and new life. In particular, it marked the start of the lambing season. The day was dedicated to the mother goddess. In Ireland this holiday later became the day of St. Brigid, the Irish saint linked to motherly qualities.

The third main Celtic festival of the year occurred on May 1. Called Beltane, it was named for Belenus, the Celtic god of fire and light. Today, this holiday is known as May Day. In the time of the ancient Celts, Beltane marked the beginning of summer. The Celts lit bonfires in celebration and led their cattle and sheep to higher pastures, where they would graze until the return of Samhain.

The final Celtic holiday was Lughnasadh. This festival was named for the sun god, Lugh. Held on August 1, Lughnasadh was largely about food. Corn and wheat, the first of the season's crops, would soon be ready. It is believed that many sacrifices took place during this ancient festival each year.[1] The Celts would kill animals such as cattle and pigs as a symbolic

The Celts held animal sacrifices to ensure a bountiful wheat harvest.

offering to the gods. In exchange for these sacrifices, the Celts hoped the gods would grant them a fruitful harvest.

Celtic religion was based on polytheism, the belief in more than one god. The Celts believed in more than 200 gods and goddesses in all. Many of them were warlike in nature. We are not certain of all their names. Until the Romans began to rule the Celts, the Celtic language was only an oral one. This means it was spoken out loud instead of written down. When the Romans began recording the Celtic language and customs, they used many of their own names in place of the Celtic ones. The Celtic sun god Lugh, for example, was thought of as being the same as Mercury. The Celtic healer and protector Nodens was likened to Mars, the Roman god of war. Sulis, the goddess of healing, became associated with Minerva, the Roman goddess of wisdom.[2] The two were connected as Sulis Minerva at the healing warm springs in Bath, England.

Celtic women had more power than other females of this time period in other cultures. Many tribes were led by women instead of men. Women even fought in Celtic battles just like men did. Celtic art often shows women and men as being the same size. Some see this similarity as a sign of equality. Celtic women also had legal rights in marriage. When a man and a woman wed, they owned their land and possessions together. When a husband or wife died, the surviving mate inherited whatever they had jointly owned. It is important to note, however, that men still had more power than women did in many ways. A husband even had the power of life or death over his wife and children.

The Celts may have been the first people to act as foster parents. As odd as the arrangement may sound to us today, members of the Celtic nobility would often send their sons to live with a different family. This foster family would then raise the boy. They agreed to teach him how to become a Celtic warrior and leader. The foster family would receive many benefits from the new relationship between the families.[3] The connection gave them higher status and more power. The noble family also benefited from the arrangement. They received the foster family's support during times of war.

The Bard by John Martin, 1817.
Bards were Celtic storytellers, who
often played the harp to accompany
their words.

The bond created between these families was based on honor. Few things were as important to the Celts as their sense of honor.

The Celtic religious leaders were the druids. In addition to being members of the clergy, these ancient druids were thought of as very wise magicians. Druids were also scholars whom the Celtic people trusted. In some cases they even acted as judges in disputes between warring chieftains. Druids ranked high in Celtic society. Some were even thought to be as powerful as kings.[4]

Also belonging to the Celtic religious system were the bards and the ovates. Bards were educated by the druids. They memorized poems and stories, often about the history of their tribes. They then retold these tales to entertain and educate the other tribe members. Ovates were the healers of the groups. They were also called seers, because they were thought to be able to look into the future.

Most of the Celts' religious ceremonies took place outdoors because Celtic religion was based so heavily in nature. They thought of the land and its waterways as being sacred. Trees and woodlands also played a huge role in Celtic mythology. These areas were considered sources of knowledge and protection.

The Celts showed great respect for their dead. This can be seen in the ornate burials given to Celtic nobility. They were far less respectful of their victims of war, however. The Celts were known as headhunters. They collected the heads of their slain enemies. They would even display them as trophies on their walls like the heads of game animals.

The Gaul Ducar decapitates Roman general Flaminius in Joseph-Noël Sylvestre's 1882 painting of the Battle of Lake Trasimene.

No one knows for sure why they did this. The purpose appears to have been rooted in their religion. The Celts believed that a person's head contained their soul.

Around the fifth century CE, the Celts began moving away from polytheism. They gradually adopted Christianity under the influence of the Romans. Like everything else the Celts did, they put their own mark on their new religion. This can be seen in Celtic crosses, which are decorated with traditional Celtic scrollwork. They also held onto some of their older legends and myths, sometimes combining them with new beliefs. What was once considered magic was now thought of as miracles.

Mystery of the Standing Stones

In various spots throughout the British Isles, groups of gargantuan stones stand upright in odd circular or oval patterns. These structures are sometimes

The Standing Stones

called megaliths because of the enormous size of the stones. Some of them stand as tall as 20 feet. Some stone circles even include ancient burial sites below the ground on which the megaliths stand.

Located in southern England, the most famous of these structures is called Stonehenge. No one knows for certain why this ancient structure was created. The most common theory is that the stones were once part of an ancient religious ceremony. Some people think they may have been used for studying astronomy. Others even believe that Stonehenge and other stone circles have magical powers.[5]

One of the biggest mysteries surrounding megaliths like Stonehenge is how these structures were created. Who placed the massive stones in their vertical positions? How did they manage it?

Many people mistakenly believe that the Celts created Stonehenge. Archaeologists have proven this theory to be impossible, though. The structure is simply too old to have been arranged by the Celts. Construction of Stonehenge may have begun as early as 3000 BCE, and it reached its final form at approximately 1600 BCE—much too early for even the brawny Celts to have placed the massive stones there.

A Roman villa at Reinheim,
the site of another important
Celtic tomb

Celtic Artwork

One of the most interesting Celtic tumuli was Reinheim. This burial site was discovered in 1954 in Germany near the border with France. The archaeologist, Josef Keller, concluded that the site was the grave of a Celtic princess, circa 300 BCE. This La Tène tomb wasn't as big as the ones at either Hochdorf or Kleinaspergle. The oak box measured only 11 feet (3.4 meters) long by 9 feet (2.7 meters) wide and was only about 3 feet (0.9 meters) deep. Most of the wood had rotted away by the time it was found. The tomb no longer contained a skeleton. Grave robbers weren't to blame, however. The soil was so acidic that it destroyed all of the bones, including the princess' teeth. This was unusual, since teeth usually survive even longer than bones.

How did Keller know the person buried here had been a princess and not a prince? The items found within the tomb told the story. The first object the team identified was the bronze handle to what may have been a mirror. An item like this would have been owned by only the richest Celts of this time period. The grave also contained many pieces of gold jewelry, bronze pins, and a bronze flagon. A disintegrated box of hundreds of amber, coral, and glass beads lay beside the jewelry that had outlasted the skeleton. The biggest clue as to the gender of the person was what was missing from the tomb: weapons. Although female Celts fought alongside male warriors, it appears that weapons were buried only with male Celts. No one knows for certain who this princess had been. She may have been the daughter of a Celtic chieftain, or she may have been the ruler of her own tribe.[1]

Artifacts like the ones found in the Reinheim tomb tell us a great deal about history. They can also be striking pieces of art in their own right. The Celts used a lot of geometric patterns to decorate their pottery and sculptures. Early Celtic artisans used many sharp lines in their designs. Chevrons and zigzagging lines are signs that a Celtic artifact is from the Hallstatt period. La Tène culture preferred fancy circles and spiral designs. One of the most popular La Tène designs is the triskele. This pattern features a triangle in the center, surrounded by three spirals. In addition to its beauty, this pattern creates the optical illusion of movement when several triskeles are arranged just right.

A triskele

When the Celts began trading with other Europeans, these new cultures had an obvious effect on Celtic art. For example, Mediterranean people often decorated their bowls and drinking cups with pictures of plant material. The lotus flower was an especially popular addition to Greek pottery. The Celts began to include pictures of plants in their own work as well. They put their own spin on the idea, though— literally. La Tène patterns combined these images with the Celts' trademark scrollwork. The stem of one leaf would often flow into a curving line that would lead into the stem of another leaf.

La Tène-styled Celtic mirror

La Tène artisans even used circles and scrolls in their pictures of people. Scrollwork actually became part of a person's face. Eyebrows, moustaches, and beards were formed out of long, fanciful curves. Even chins and noses are circular. The faces shown on Celtic pottery didn't look realistic, but that wasn't the point. They had large, round eyes and faces that showed little expression. They weren't meant to look like real faces.

Some historians think the faces in Celtic art were meant to look like they were guards of some sort. This may be why the Celts wore items with these images on them into battle. Perhaps the warriors believed that these symbols had protective powers. Other historians think that Celtic art was a form of religious expression. They think that the faces and other symbols represent the Celtic gods and goddesses.

Mistletoe was another plant the Celts pictured in their art. They used the leaves of this plant as medicine in everyday life. It was thought to be a powerful remedy for many ailments. At first glance mistletoe leaves may look like giant ears on the head of a person in Celtic artwork. Some

Mistletoe

historians believe that mistletoe leaves in Celtic art are the sign of an extremely honored person. They think the Celts used these leaves the way Christians used halos in their paintings of saints.[2]

In Celtic artwork everything is connected. Circles and plants flow into the faces of people. Animals are also part of these merging pictures. They are often shown with human faces that look like masks. It can be difficult to tell exactly where one image ends and others begin. Wings, for example, may be placed between a human and an owl, touching both beings. From one perspective the wings look like they belong to the animal. From another they seem to be part of the person.

Birds are commonly pictured on Celtic works of art. Fibulas are among the most commonly found artifacts in tumuli. These primitive clothes fasteners usually have some sort of bird on them. Triskeles often include images of birds.

Sculptures of horses are also fairly common. Some parts of the animal are unmistakable, whereas others don't seem to belong to it at all.

One of the most fascinating aspects of art is that each person may see it differently. No one knows for certain what all the imagery in Celtic art means. The more pieces we discover and study, however, the more we can learn about how the Celts used these items. We can also make educated guesses as to what they were trying to say through their designs.

Celtic Clothing

Celts wore a variety of clothing, but some items were more common than others. Men wore pants called bracae, or breeches, and tunic-style linen shirts. Women wore longer tunic-style dresses called peplos. Many of these Celtic pieces of clothing looked similar to clothing worn by the Greeks. The biggest

Celtic clothing

difference was in the fabrics. Celts' clothes were made from more colorful, heavier, and rougher cloth.

Both men and women wore heavy woolen cloaks called laenae. These cloaks were usually woven into plaid prints. These designs, called tartans, are still popular in Ireland and Scotland today. The combination of colors in a Celt's tartan was unique to his or her clan. The weight of a cloak and the brooches used for fastening them also said something about the clan. The wealthiest clans had the very best cloaks. The quality of Celtic cloaks was so high that these items were in great demand all the way to Rome. They were among the most popular items imported into the city.[3]

The Celts enjoyed dressing in bright colors. Women were responsible for dyeing the fabrics using berries, seaweed, and other types of plants. Most Celtic clothing was made from wool, but some Celts wore items made from linen and silk. Although silk was created in Asia, it was traded throughout Europe. The Celts were known to unravel old silk clothes and make new cloth out of them.

Rome's Capitoline Hill today. More than 2,000 years ago it was the site of a months-long struggle between invading Celts and the Romans.

CHAPTER 5

The Legacy of the Ancient Celts

Historians disagree about the reason the Celts kept expanding their territory. Some argue that Celts needed more land for their growing population. Others insist that greed had just as much to do with it. The Celts were known for being extremely brave in battle. This reputation was important to the Celts. The more land they invaded, the larger their territory became.

Thus the Celts became well established in northern Italy, and some modern cities in that region may have Celtic origins. Eventually they came into conflict with the rising power of Rome. In 390 BCE the Celts invaded the Estruscan town of Clusium and demanded land. Clusium asked for help from Rome. The Celts attacked the Roman army that responded and defeated them, then proceeded to march on Rome itself.

At first it looked like the Celts were winning. Before they got to the fortress on Capitoline Hill, though, the Romans rallied their forces. They were not simply going to surrender this important defensive position. The fighting went on for several months. During this time the Celts looted the areas surrounding the city. They also killed many civilians and burned many homes to the ground.

Finally the Romans decided they would try bargaining with the Celts. The Romans agreed to pay the Celts 1,000 pounds of gold to leave their city. The Celts accepted the terms, but they did not go quietly. When the

Romans complained about how the Celts were weighing the gold, the Celtic commander became angry. He lay his sword down on top of the pile. "Vae victus!" he proclaimed, which meant "Woe to the defeated!"[1]

Just at this moment, according to one version, another Roman army arrived. Its general was not pleased with the agreement that was taking place. He told the people, "With iron, and not with gold, Rome buys her freedom."[2] By this he meant that the Romans would fight for peace by using their weapons instead of bribing the Celts with riches. Another battle followed. This time the Romans won. They saved their city and drove the Celts far north of Rome. According to another version, the Celts accepted the money and departed.

The Celts may have lost their battle for Rome, but they held onto their reputation for being brave warriors. Many Celts worked as mercenaries, or hired soldiers, during this time. Some even fought for people who had been their enemies in the past. About a century after the battle that began the Celts' war with the Romans, the Celts were fighting alongside the Etruscans against Rome.[3]

By 323 BCE the Celts had moved eastward into Greece. Historians also disagree about exactly what took place during this time. Some say that the Greeks defeated the barbarians, as the Celts were known. Others believe the Celts defeated the Greeks and left with great treasure. Whichever account is correct, several clans continued to move to the east. They raided numerous cities in the process.

The Celts' expansion continued until around 233 BCE, when an army from Pergamum in western Asia Minor led by Attalus I was sent to Greece to fight the Celts. This army defeated the Celts, and the victory was widely celebrated. At the same time, the Romans were regaining control of the areas they had once controlled. They were also expanding their own empire. Warring between the Romans and the Celts continued on and off for the next three centuries. It did not end for good until Julius Caesar defeated the Celts around 51 BCE.[4]

It took Caesar more than eight years to conquer the Celts. In the end it was his strategy of dividing the Celts that made all the difference. He used the Celtic clans' inability to work together to separate them into less menacing groups. Certain clans would fight against other clans, essentially helping Caesar's legions. In this way he was able to defeat the Celtic clans one at a time.

What Caesar feared more than the individual clans were the druid leaders. He worried that they could unite the Celts through religion. Fortunately for Caesar, this never happened. Nearly 100 years later, an emperor of Rome named Claudius attacked the druids. In 43 CE, he ordered an invasion of Britain, where 14 different Celtic tribes still existed. Claudius' men killed all the druid priests before they could unite the Celts, but it took the emperor 40 more years to overpower the remaining Celts. Yet revolts continued. Another Roman emperor, Hadrian, built a protective wall across northern Britain in 122 CE.

Hadrian's Wall

Proclaiming Claudius Emperor by 19th century English painter Sir Lawrence Alma-Tadema

Although the Celts were no longer in control, they did not simply adopt all of the Romans' ways. Celtic culture continued through the people's art, language, and music. Of course, Celtic culture after Caesar and Claudius was greatly influenced by the Romans. This new way of life was a combination of ancient Celtic lore and the new era that was emerging.

Celtic Culture Lives On

Today people from all around the world are still drawn to Celtic culture. Celtic folklore is considered one of the most interesting parts of British and European history. Because the Celts lived in so many different

Celtic Woman

areas, tourists can learn about Celtic history in numerous regions of Europe. The Celtic legacy is very important to people from these regions.

Celtic music and dance are especially popular today. The Irish stage show Riverdance and the all-female singing group called Celtic Woman both arose from Celtic culture. We do not know for certain whether today's Celtic music sounds anything like the melodies played by the ancient Celts. Whatever its sound, it is likely that original Celtic music varied somewhat from region to region. Contemporary Celtic music does as well. English, Irish, and Scottish versions of this musical style are all a bit different.

In the United States, Celtic culture is revered. Groups that study and re-enact Celtic history abound on both sides of the Atlantic Ocean. Members gather together with their families to live like the Celts—at least for a little while. On weekends, for instance, re-enactors will travel to a remote location. Once there they dress in Celtic clothing, prepare Celtic foods, and dance and sing along with Celtic music. Many members even speak in Celtic dialects and re-enact famous battles. People don't have to be members to attend these events. Many groups hold fairs where the general public can join in some of the fun.

Design Your Own Celtic Knot

Among the most popular Celtic decorations are Celtic knots. These designs may be extremely simple or very intricate. You can put these Celtic symbols on virtually anything.

MATERIALS

- Pencil
- Black permanent marker
- Colored fabric markers
- Iron-on transfer paper
- Fabric item of your choice

DIRECTIONS

1. Practice drawing your own Celtic knot.
   You can find drawings of Celtic knots online, or you may design your own.
2. Once you have chosen a design you like, you may need to resize it. You can use a photocopier or computer scanner to increase or decrease the size of your design. Some of these machines will even print your design to fit your specific dimensions of the item on which you want your Celtic knot to appear.
3. Next, trace your design onto special paper from the craft store that will allow you to transfer the pattern onto a piece of fabric. You can place the design on a t-shirt, a tote bag, or even multiple squares of cloth to make a Celtic quilt.

4. Once you have transferred the pattern, you can add color to the design with fabric markers.

Ancient Recipe: Bread and Butter Pudding

At the time of the Celts, this dessert would have been made with dense soda bread. It also might have included nuts and berries gathered by the female clan members.

INGREDIENTS

7 slices of bread
Soft butter
4 cups milk
3 eggs, slightly beaten
½ cup sugar
¼ teaspoon salt
½ cup raisins
1 teaspoon vanilla
½ teaspoon cinnamon

DIRECTIONS

1. Preheat oven to 325 degrees Fahrenheit. Butter a 2-quart baking dish.
2. Generously butter each slice of bread on one side. Place as many slices as will fit into the bottom of the baking dish, butter-side up. Set remaining buttered slices aside.
3. Mix remaining ingredients. Pour mixture over bread slices. Top with remaining buttered slices, butter-side up. Press the top slices down a bit until they are all soaking in the milk mixture.
4. Let stand for at least 10 minutes. If the bread is dry, wait a bit longer.
5. Cover and bake for 30 minutes. Remove the cover and continue to bake for another 30 minutes. Turn on broiler for the last few minutes, or until the top turns a deep golden color.
6. Serve warm with heavy cream.

BCE

ca. 3300	The Bronze Age begins.
ca. 1600	Stonehenge is completed.
ca. 1300	The Iron Age begins.
800	The Hallstatt period of Celtic culture begins.
ca. 550	The Hochdorf tomb is constructed.
500	Greek historian Hecataeus makes the first known written reference to the Celts.
450	La Tène A period begins.
390	The Celts begin a siege of Rome. La Tène B period begins.
300	La Tène C period begins.
ca. 300	The Reinheim tomb is created.

279	The Celts invade Greece but are driven back.
233	Attalus I of Pergamum defeats the Celts in Greece.
75	La Tène D period begins.
52	Julius Caesar defeats the Celts in the Battle of Alesia.
CE	
43	Roman emperor Claudius invades Britain to conquer the Celts living there.
ca. 400	Christianity is introduced to Ireland.
476	The Roman Empire collapses.
1879	Oscar Fraas discovers the Kleinaspergle tomb.
1954	Josef Keller discovers the Reinheim tomb.
1977	Jörg Biel discovers the Hochdorf tomb.

Celtic graves

Chapter 1: An Exciting Discovery

1. Barry Cunliffe, *The Ancient Celts* (London, England: Penguin Books, 1997), p. 57.
2. "The First Europeans," *Christian History,* 1998, Volume 17, Issue 4, p. 2.
3. "History According to Salt," *Time,* March 15, 1982, Volume 119, Issue 11, p. 58.

Chapter 2: The Development of the Ancient Celts

1. Edward H. Heffner, "Archaeological Discussions," *American Journal of Archaeology,* July–December 1930.
2. Miranda Green, *The Celtic World* (London, England: Routledge, 1995), p. 8.
3. Doreen Waugh, "Dialects of English: Northern and Insular Scots," *Scottish Language,* 2007, Issue 26, pp. 96–98.

Chapter 3: Celtic Beliefs

1. Miranda Green, *The Celtic World* (London, England: Routeledge, 1995), p. 438.
2. Louise Revell, "Religion and Ritual in the Western Provinces," Greece & Rome, 2007, Volume 54, Issue 2, pp. 210–228.
3. Barry Cunliffe, *The Ancient Celts,* (London, England: Penguin Books, 1997), pp. 108–109.
4. Robert Harbison, "The Philosopher and the Druids: A Journey Among the Ancient Celts," *Library Journal,* December 15, 2005, Volume 130, Issue 20, p. 145.
5. William Underhill, "Putting Stonehenge In Its Place," *Scientific American,* March 2011, Volume 304, Issue 3, pp. 48–53.

Chapter 4: Celtic Artwork

1. Miranda Green, *The Celtic World* (London, England: Routledge, 1995), p. 300.
2. Andrea Brewer Shea and David Duhl, "Myths and Lore of Mistletoe," *The Tennessee Conservationist,* November/December 1997.
3. Carol Vogel, "Tartan Touches," *New York Times Magazine,* March 11, 1990, p. 70.

Chapter 5: The Legacy of the Celts

1. New World Celts, http://www.newworldcelts.org/index.php?option=com_content&view=category&layout=blog&id=29&Itemid=42
2. National Gallery of Art, http://www.nga.gov/collection/gallery/gg7/gg7-294.html
3. Barry Cunliffe, *The Ancient Celts* (London, England: Penguin Books, 1997), p. 217.
4. Atlas of World History, http://atlasofworldhistory.com/NATIONS/Celts.html

Further Reading

Works Consulted

Cunliffe, Barry. *The Ancient Celts.* London: Penguin Books, 1997.

Green, Miranda. *The Celtic World.* London: Routledge, 1995.

King, John. *Kingdoms of the Celts.* London: Blanford, 1998.

University of Texas at Austin, "Iron Age Celts – Reinheim (Saarland), Germany" http://www.laits.utexas.edu/ironagecelts/reinheim.php

Books

Green, Jen. *National Geographic Investigates: Ancient Celts: Archaeology Unlocks the Secrets of the Celts' Past.* Washington, DC: National Geographic Children's Books, 2008.

Hinds, Kathryn. *Barbarians: Ancient Celts.* Tarrytown, New York: Marshall Cavendish Children's Books, 2009.

Leslie, Clare Walker. *The Ancient Celtic Festivals and How We Celebrate Them Today.* Rochester, Vermont: Inner Traditions, 2008.

MacDonald, Fiona. *Step into the Celtic World.* London: Anness, 2010.

Meyer, Jane G. *The Life of Saint Brigid – Abbess of Kildare.* Chesterton, Indiana: Conciliar Press, 2009.

On the Internet

BBC: Build an Iron Age House
http://www.bbc.co.uk/history/interactive/animations/ironage_roundhouse/index.shtml

Celtic Culture
http://www.celtic-culture.com/

Iron Age Celts
http://www.bbc.co.uk/wales/celts/

Iron Age Celts
http://celts.mrdonn.org/

Tales of the Celts
http://www.chalicecentre.net/stories.htm

archaeologist (ahr-kee-AWL-uh-jist)—A person who studies earlier times through artifacts and fossils.

artifact (AHR-tuh-fakt)—A humanmade object.

barbarian (bahr-BAIR-ee-uhn)—A person without culture, education, or civility; a savage.

bard (BAHRD)—A person who recites poems and stories, often while playing music.

bracae (brah-KAY)—Pants or breeches worn by Celtic men.

chieftain (CHEEF-tuhn)—The leader of a Celtic clan.

civilian (si-VIL-yun)—A person who is not part of the military.

cloak (CLOHK)—A loose coat or cape.

dialect (DY-uh-lekt)—A variety of a language spoken in a specific area.

druid (DROO-id)—A leader of a certain pre-Christian religion.

fibula (FIB-yoo-luh)—Ornamented clasp used to fasten clothing.

flagon (FLAG-uhn)—A large container for drinks such as water or wine.

hearse (HURSE)—A vehicle used to carry a dead person.

kylikes (KAHY-lix)—A shallow drinking cup with two handles.

laenae (luh-NAY)—Heavy woolen cloaks.

loot (LOOT)—To carry off or steal.

mercenaries (MUR-suh-ner-eez)—Hired soldiers.

migrate (MY-grate)—To move from one region to another.

mint (MINT)—To make money by stamping coins from metal.

ovate (OH-veyt)—A Celtic healer, thought to be a prophet.

peplos (PEP-luhs)—A long, tunic-style dress.

polytheism (pahl-ee-THEE-iz-uhm)—The belief in more than one god.

sacrifice (SAK-ruh-fhys)—The act of offering an animal, person, or item to a god; also the animal, person, or item being offered.

symposium (sim-POH-zee-uhm)—A Greek drinking party.

tartan (TAHR-tuhn)—A plaid print, often associated with a specific clan.

technology (tek-NOL-uh-jee)—The means by which a group of people makes tools and other items they need.

triskele (trih-SKEL)—A La Téne design made up of a triangle surrounded by spirals.

tumuli (TOO-myuh-ly)—Mounds of earth containing a burial site.

Index

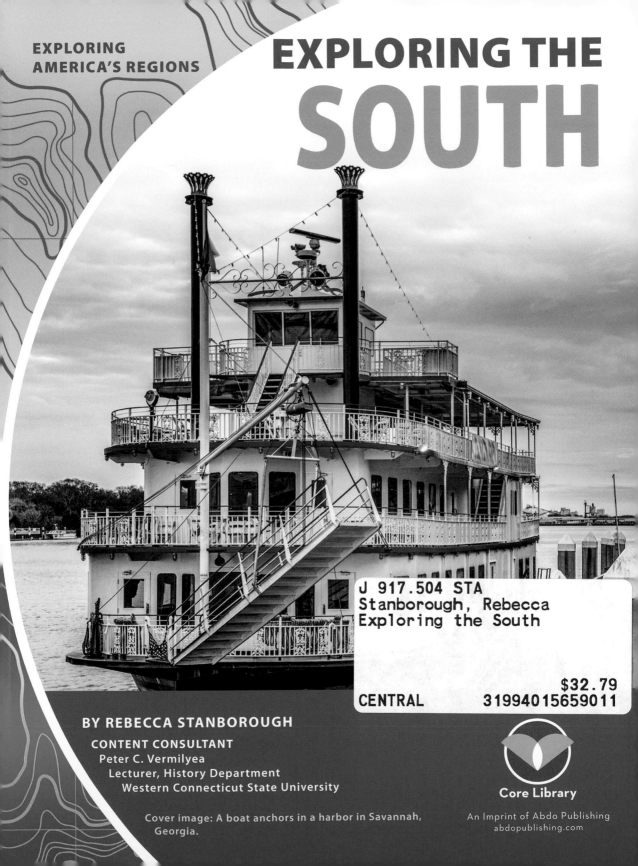

EXPLORING
AMERICA'S REGIONS

EXPLORING THE
SOUTH

BY REBECCA STANBOROUGH

CONTENT CONSULTANT
Peter C. Vermilyea
Lecturer, History Department
Western Connecticut State University

Cover image: A boat anchors in a harbor in Savannah,
Georgia.

Core Library

An Imprint of Abdo Publishing
abdopublishing.com

abdopublishing.com

Published by Abdo Publishing, a division of ABDO, PO Box 398166, Minneapolis, Minnesota 55439. Copyright © 2018 by Abdo Consulting Group, Inc. International copyrights reserved in all countries. No part of this book may be reproduced in any form without written permission from the publisher. Core Library™ is a trademark and logo of Abdo Publishing.

Printed in the United States of America, North Mankato, Minnesota
092017
012018

Cover Photo: Sean Pavone/Shutterstock Images
Interior Photos: Sean Pavone/Shutterstock Images, 1; Shutterstock Images, 4–5, 24–25, 30–31, 45; Jon Bilous/Shutterstock Images, 7; Red Line Editorial, 9, 29; Luc Novovitch/Alamy, 10–11; Robert Abbott Sengstacke/Archive Photos/Getty Images, 14; MSFC/NASA, 16; Melinda Fawver/Shutterstock Images, 18–19, 43; Bruce Ellis/Shutterstock Images, 22; Steve Bower/Shutterstock Images, 28; Stephen Searle/Alamy, 34; Ralph Notaro/Getty Images Entertainment/Getty Images, 36–37

Editor: Maddie Spalding
Imprint Designer: Maggie Villaume
Series Design Direction: Ryan Gale

Publisher's Cataloging-in-Publication Data

Names: Stanborough, Rebecca, author.
Title: Exploring the South / by Rebecca Stanborough.
Description: Minneapolis, Minnesota : Abdo Publishing, 2018. | Series: Exploring America's regions | Includes online resources and index.
Identifiers: LCCN 2017946946 | ISBN 9781532113833 (lib.bdg.) | ISBN 9781532152719 (ebook)
Subjects: LCSH: Southern States--Juvenile literature. | Discovery and exploration--Juvenile literature. | Travel--Juvenile literature. | United States--Historical geography--Juvenile literature.
Classification: DDC 917.5--dc23
LC record available at https://lccn.loc.gov/2017946946

CONTENTS

WELCOME TO THE SOUTH

The South is a region of varied landscapes and attractions. Canoers seek out wildlife in Louisiana's bayous. Hikers explore mountain chains such as the Great Smoky Mountains. Thrill seekers roar through the Florida Everglades on open airboats. The South is so vast and the weather is so warm that adventures can be found year-round.

The South includes 12 states. Virginia, North Carolina, South Carolina, Georgia, and Florida all border the Atlantic Ocean. Florida also borders the Gulf of Mexico, a large Atlantic Ocean basin. Louisiana, Mississippi,

Visitors explore the Everglades in an open airboat.

and Alabama border the Gulf of Mexico as well. Arkansas, Tennessee, Kentucky, and West Virginia are landlocked states.

The landscape of the South is varied. In some states, such as Georgia and West Virginia, trees cover much of the land. Florida, on the other hand, is full of lakes, rivers, and marshes. Florida's Everglades are the largest subtropical wetland ecosystem in North America.

THE CLIMATE OF THE SOUTH

The southern climate is generally warm and sunny with mild winters. In summer, the weather becomes

WELCOME, Y'ALL!

Perhaps the most famous southern slang word is "y'all." It is used to address more than one person. It is a contraction of "you all." But where did the word come from? Some scholars say it came from the Scots-Irish phrase "ye aw." "Ye aw" appears in a letter written by a Scotsman in 1737. Many people came to the South from Scotland and Ireland in the 1700s. Other scholars say the word came from enslaved African Americans in the South.

The state of West Virginia has fairly mountainous terrain.

hot and humid. Throughout the summer and fall, southern states along the Atlantic Ocean might be hit by hurricanes. A hurricane is a system of spiraling winds that forms over an ocean. Hurricanes can build in strength as they travel across the ocean until they hit land along the coast. Hurricanes can cause flooding that damages roads and buildings.

SHOULD PRINCEVILLE REBUILD?

In October 2016, Hurricane Matthew slammed the Atlantic coastline in the South. Students in Princeville, North Carolina, were forced to attend a temporary school. Their school flooded during the hurricane. It also flooded during Hurricane Floyd in 1999. Some people argue that everyone should leave Princeville. But the town has a special history. It is said to be the first US town built by freed African-American slaves. Mayor Bobbie Jones said, "The freed slaves made it what it is . . . I'm fighting so hard to make sure Princeville is not one of the casualties. It would be a devastating tragedy, not only for me, but for the world."

Although much of the South is warm throughout the year, the climate may vary in areas with higher elevations. Snow falls in mountainous areas. Some places get enough snow to make skiing possible.

The South encompasses varied landscapes, from beaches to mountains. Millions of people visit this region each year. The South welcomes people who want to explore its rich landscapes and culture.

THE SOUTHERN
REGION

The map below shows the states, the capitals, and some of the major cities that make up the South. After reading about this region, what did you think it would look like? Based on the location of these states, what kinds of plants and animals do you think might be common in the South?

HISTORY AND SETTLEMENT

Native Americans lived in the South hundreds of years before European settlers arrived. The Cherokee, Chickasaw, and Shawnee people live mainly in Oklahoma today. But their original homelands encompassed parts of the South. Cherokee people lived in a region that includes present-day Tennessee, North Carolina, and South Carolina. The Choctaw and Chickasaw nations lived in a region that includes present-day Alabama and Mississippi. The Creek people lived in present-day Georgia and Alabama. The Shawnee people settled around the Appalachian Mountains

Cherokee men perform a traditional dance at an event in Cherokee, North Carolina.

HONORING TRADITIONS

Lewis J. Johnson is an assistant chief of the Seminole Nation. In a 2013 interview, he described why he believes it is important for the Seminole people to maintain their cultures and traditions. He said: "I remember a time when going to a traditional Indian church or attending the traditional ceremonial grounds was not necessarily something you participated in because it was your choice. It was done because it was who you were. You actively involved yourself because it was what you did as member of the Seminole community. Times may be changing, but where culture and spirituality thrive becomes the place where we will survive."

in the South. They lived in an area that includes present-day Alabama, Tennessee, and Kentucky. In what is now southern Florida, Seminole tribes occupied large areas of land. Present-day Louisiana was home to the Natchez tribes.

Explorers from Spain began arriving in the South in the 1500s. Later, explorers from England and France arrived in the area. Native Americans had been living in the region for many generations. The settlers took away lands that belonged to the Native American people.

SLAVERY AND THE CIVIL WAR

Beginning in the 1600s, European settlers and their descendants enslaved people from Africa and forced them to work on large farms in the South called plantations. Many were enslaved on plantations that grew cotton, sugarcane, or tobacco.

By the 1800s, people in the North and the South often held different views on slavery. The South wanted to keep slavery legal. But many people in the North had

THE TRAIL OF TEARS

In 1830, President Andrew Jackson signed the Indian Removal Act. It allowed US officials to take control of Native American lands. The law forced many Native Americans to move to land west of the Mississippi River. In 1838 and 1839, approximately 15,000 Cherokee people were forced to march to Oklahoma. More than 4,000 of them died on the journey. This forced march is known as The Trail of Tears. Few Cherokee were left in the South as a result.

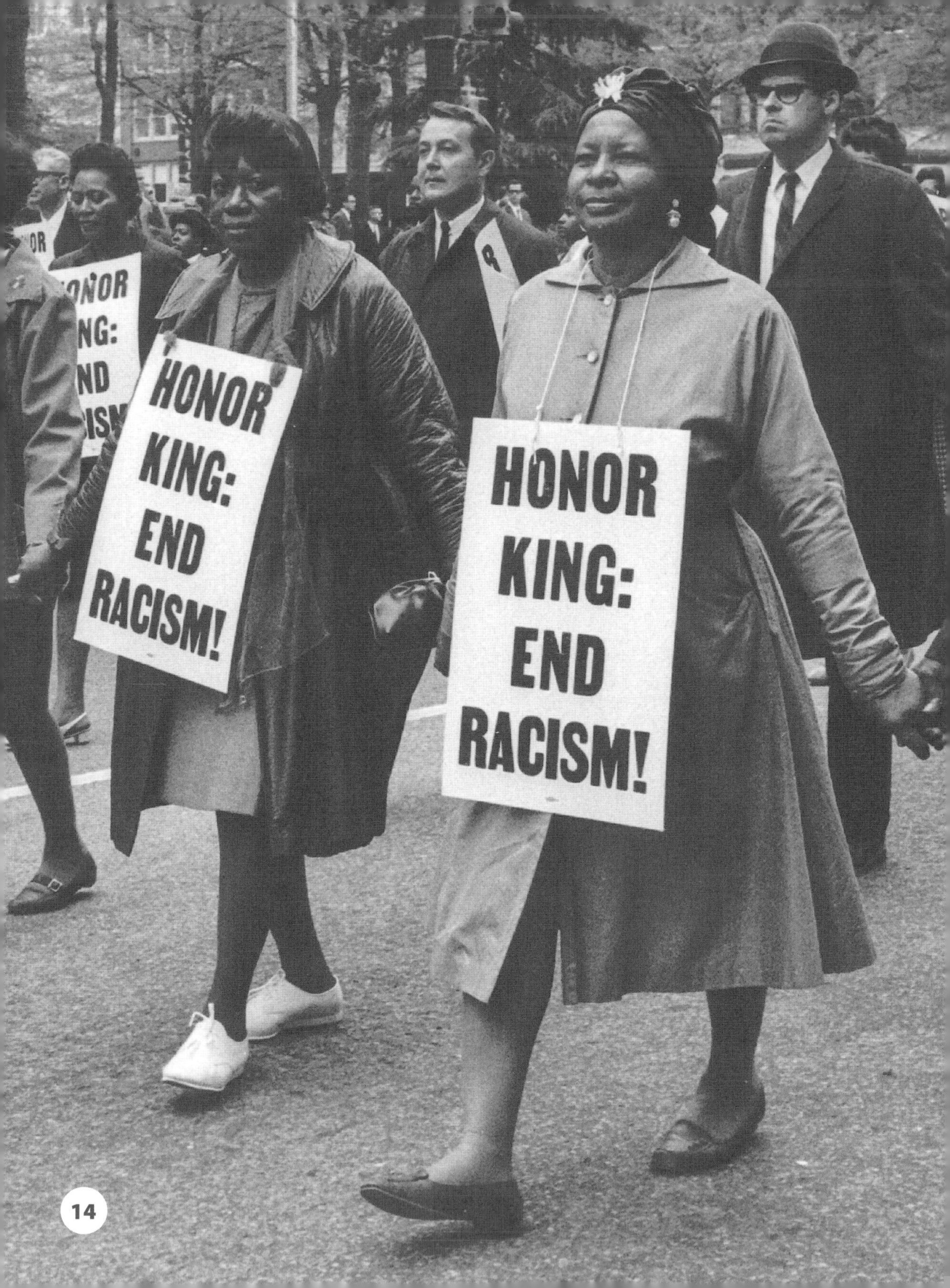
HONOR
KING:
END
RACISM!
HONOR
KING:
END
RACISM!

come to believe that slavery was wrong. The southern states decided to leave the Union. This resulted in the Civil War (1861–1865). The southern, or Confederate, states lost the war. They were brought back into the Union. Enslaved people were eventually freed.

Even after slavery ended, life for most African Americans in the South was difficult. A system of laws enforced segregation, the separation of African Americans and European Americans. Better jobs, schools, homes, and services were given to European Americans. African Americans were denied the right to vote. They were intimidated with violence and even death. But many African Americans, such as activist Martin Luther King Jr., fought back. They protested. In 1964, President Lyndon B. Johnson signed the Civil Rights Act. This act outlawed segregation.

People marched in 1968 after Martin Luther King Jr.'s death to protest racism.

Astronaut Buzz Aldrin steps out of the Apollo 11 spacecraft onto the moon in 1969.

THE MODERN ERA

The South is the site of several historic advances. Wilbur and Orville Wright made the first successful airplane flight in Kitty Hawk, North Carolina, in 1903. Approximately 65 years later, another flight milestone was reached in the South. The Apollo 11 mission launched from Florida's Kennedy Space Center in 1969. After leaving Earth's orbit, the spacecraft landed on the moon. The Apollo 11 astronauts Buzz Aldrin and Neil Armstrong were the first people to walk on the moon.

STRAIGHT TO THE
SOURCE

John Lewis is an African-American civil rights leader and politician from Alabama. On August 28, 1963, he gave a speech to protestors in Washington, DC. He said:

> To those who have said, "Be patient and wait," we must say that we cannot be patient. We do not want our freedom gradually, but we want to be free now! We are tired. We are tired of being beaten by policemen. We are tired of seeing our people locked up in jail over and over again. . . . We do not want to go to jail. But we will go to jail if this is the price we must pay for love, brotherhood, and true peace. I appeal to all of you to get into this great revolution that is sweeping this nation. Get in and stay in the streets of every city, every village and hamlet of this nation until true freedom comes.

> Source: John Lewis. "Speech at the March on Washington." *Voices of Democracy: The US Oratory Project.* Student Nonviolent Coordinating Committee Papers, August 28, 1963. Web. Accessed July 18, 2017.

Consider Your Audience

Adapt this passage for a different audience, such as your friends. Write a blog post conveying this same information for the new audience. How does your post differ from the original text, and why?

CHAPTER
THREE

FAMOUS LANDMARKS

The South is home to many of the nation's best-known landmarks. The largest mountain range in the region is the Appalachian Mountains. They include the Great Smoky Mountains and Blue Ridge Mountains. The Great Smoky Mountains stretch across Tennessee and North Carolina. The Blue Ridge Mountains cross through the states of North Carolina, South Carolina, Virginia, and Georgia.

Kentucky's Mammoth Cave is the longest system of underground caves in the world. It consists of more than 400 miles (644 km)

Great Smoky Mountains National Park is the most-visited US national park.

of caverns. Mammoth Cave is part of a karst system. Karst is underground rock that has been worn away, creating sinkholes and caves that store water.

The longest river in the South is the Mississippi River. It is 2,350 miles (3,782 km) long. It begins in Minnesota. From there, it travels south. It winds through Kentucky, Tennessee, Arkansas, Mississippi, and Louisiana. In Louisiana, the river empties into the Gulf of Mexico. Along the river's route, the soil is often good for farming because floodwaters leave rich minerals behind. The river's floodplain is known as the Mississippi Delta.

Another major landmark in the South is the Florida Everglades. The Everglades are sometimes called the River of Grass. The Everglades are made up of 1.5 million acres (607,029 ha) of wetlands. Everglades National Park serves as a wildlife refuge.

MAN-MADE LANDMARKS

One of the most well-known man-made landmarks in the South is Monticello. Monticello is the home of former president Thomas Jefferson. Monticello is located in Charlottesville, Virginia.

FORT SUMTER

Fort Sumter was built on a man-made island off the coast of South Carolina in the 1800s. The fort is equipped with 135 cannons. It was meant to protect Charleston harbor from invaders. In 1861, the Confederate army fired on Fort Sumter. This event triggered the Civil War. Though it was nearly demolished in the war, today Fort Sumter has been restored. It is a national monument.

Monticello is a well-known historic site in the South.

The home was built and maintained by people Jefferson had enslaved. More than 160 different kinds of trees were planted on the grounds. The United Nations has named Monticello a World Heritage Site because of its history and the landscaping of its architecture and grounds.

The Pentagon is another important man-made landmark. This huge, five-sided building is located in Arlington, Virginia. The Pentagon is the home of the US Department of Defense. The Department of Defense is in charge of protecting the United States. It includes all branches of the United States armed forces.

EXPLORE ONLINE

Chapter Three describes Monticello, Thomas Jefferson's home. People Jefferson enslaved built Monticello. Jefferson said, "My first wish is that the labourers may be well-treated." On the Monticello website, you can read about how Jefferson's enslaved workers were actually treated. What evidence can you find that they were not treated well?

THE THOMAS JEFFERSON FOUNDATION
abdocorelibrary.com/exploring-south

PLANTS AND ANIMALS

Because the South encompasses varied landscapes, its plant and animal life is diverse. The largest wild animal in the region is the black bear. Black bears can be found in mountains and forests throughout the South. They typically eat nuts, berries, insects, and fish.

Coastal wetlands in the South are home to approximately 5 million American alligators. Many alligators live in the freshwater swamps and marshes of the Everglades. Alligators are the largest reptiles in North America.

An alligator rests in the swamps of Everglades National Park.

Manatees live along Florida's coast in the Gulf of Mexico and the Atlantic Ocean. They are sometimes called sea cows because of their size and eating habits. Manatees eat underwater plants. In winter, they migrate to warm springs and rivers in Florida. They cannot survive in temperatures below 68 degrees Fahrenheit (20°C).

Many species of birds also live in the South. Flamingos are common wading birds in coastal zones. Flamingos almost disappeared from the United States in the late 1800s. Settlers

THE EYELESS CAVE FISH

The eyeless cave fish lives in sinkholes in Mammoth Cave. This fish has evolved so that it no longer has eyes. Scientists studied blind cave fish in Mexico to learn how they find food. The scientists discovered that the fish's skull bones are not the same size on both sides. These fish swim in the same direction all the time. This pattern helps them find food more often than if they swam randomly. Constantly swimming in one direction causes the bones on one side to bend as the fish grows.

harvested their feathers and eggs. In recent years, small flocks have returned.

PLANTS OF THE SOUTH

Perhaps the best-known plants in the South are those that bloom in the spring. Magnolia trees have shiny leaves and white flowers. They can grow 60 to 80 feet (18 to 24 m) tall. Magnolias grow wild across the South.

Coastal zones in the South are home to

Mangrove trees grow along the coast in the South.

mangrove and banyan trees. Mangroves are short trees with roots that can be seen above the ground. Banyan trees are sometimes called "strangler figs." They grow on top of other trees. Banyan trees have roots that grow down through the air from branches.

MANATEE RANGE
MAP

This map shows where manatees live. How can you tell from this map that manatees live in warm water habitats? Where else do manatees live besides the Florida coast?

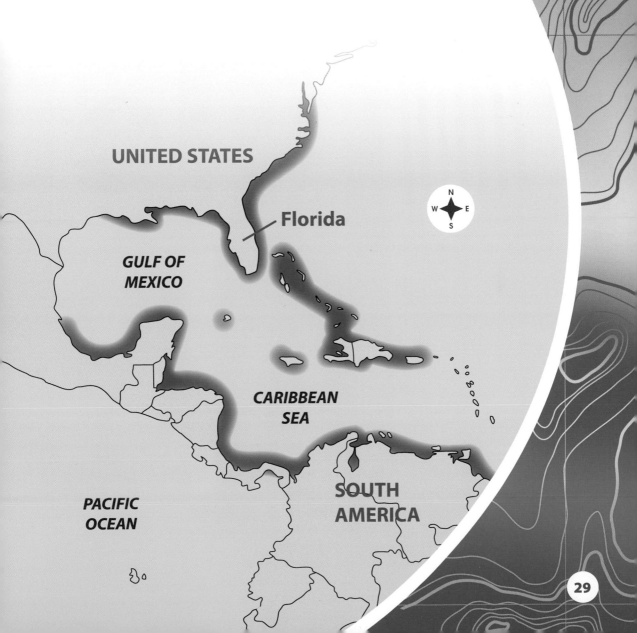

UNITED STATES

Florida

GULF OF
MEXICO

CARIBBEAN
SEA

PACIFIC
OCEAN

SOUTH
AMERICA

WORKING IN THE SOUTH

The South is the fastest-growing region by population in the nation. One reason for that growth is the South's strong economy. Agribusiness, aerospace, and tourism are some of the region's biggest industries.

AGRIBUSINESS

The South has long been a major source of crops that feed the nation. Farmers also grow fibers such as cotton to make clothing and fabrics. But agribusiness is more than just farming. It also includes forestry. Forestry is the business of growing and harvesting trees

Inside Kennedy Space Center's Vehicle Assembly Building, workers build rockets.

for timber. Agribusiness also includes the production of meat. Georgia is the top producer of chickens in the United States. The state produces more than 1 billion chickens each year. North Carolina is one of the top producers of pork in the nation.

AEROSPACE

The aerospace industry employs many people in the South. Commercial and military airplanes are built in South Carolina. The National Aeronautics and Space Administration (NASA) has centers for space research across the region. Stennis Space Center in Mississippi is NASA's main rocket engine testing facility. At NASA's Langley Research Center in Virginia, scientists study everything from biofuels to drones. Parts of the International Space Station, a laboratory orbiting Earth, were built at Marshall Space Center in Huntsville, Alabama. And scientists at Kennedy Space Center in Florida launch and test rockets.

TOURISM

Every year, millions of people vacation in the South. Florida is home to Walt Disney World, a theme park that celebrates the legacy of animator Walt Disney. Tourism is

SOUTH CAROLINA'S FUTURE SCIENTISTS

South Carolina's aerospace industry is among the top in the nation. To make sure students are prepared for jobs in this growing field, the state created high school aerospace programs. Students in these programs study the design and flight of aircraft and spacecraft. Similar aerospace engineering programs are taking off in schools in North Carolina, West Virginia, and Alabama.

Musicians march in a parade at Walt Disney World in Florida.

Florida's biggest industry. Tourism is also one of South Carolina's top industries. People are drawn to South Carolina's beaches and to historic cities such as Charleston. Tourism brings in approximately $20 billion each year to South Carolina. Tourists create thousands of jobs for people who live in the South.

STRAIGHT TO THE
SOURCE

Lake Lanier in Georgia connects to other lakes and rivers that flow south to the Gulf of Mexico. Many farmers in the South rely on this river system for clean water. Florida native Jim McClellan describes why the Apalachicola River in this river system should be protected:

> There was a time when the river could be all things to all people: a drinking water supply for our neighbors to the north, a transportation system linking the mountains to the sea and a source of recreation and sustenance for everyone fortunate enough to live along its path. That time has passed. Now we have to choose which of those things deserves our greatest efforts to protect. . . . One way can take us to a sustainable, healthy river system; the other will leave us high and dry.

> Source: Jessie Thomas-Blate. "Less Water for them is Inconvenient; Less for the River is Catastrophic." *American Rivers*. American Rivers, April 21, 2016. Web. Accessed May 26, 2017.

Back It Up

The author of this passage is using evidence to support a point. Write a paragraph describing the point the author is making. Then write down two or three pieces of evidence the author uses to make the point.

PEOPLES AND CULTURES

The music, food, and traditions of the South tell the story of the many people who have lived in the region. The South is home to many Native Americans. Some members of the Choctaw Nation live in Mississippi. Descendants of the Creek people live in Alabama. The Seminole Tribe of Florida has more than 2,000 members.

Today, the largest population groups in the South are the descendants of European

Seminole people celebrate their heritage at the Seminole Tribal Fair & Pow Wow in Florida.

settlers and African Americans. Immigrants from Mexico and other Spanish-speaking countries are the fastest-growing population group. Southern culture is becoming richer and more interesting because of its growing diversity.

SOUTHERN MUSIC

Some of the most iconic American musical genres, such as the blues, were born in the South. Music scholars say that blues music has its roots in the songs of enslaved African Americans. Blues music shares singing patterns with music from parts of Africa. One such pattern is "call and response." Someone sings a line, and the audience sings something in response. Blues lyrics often speak about hard times.

Jazz was also born in the South. Jazz has its roots in African-American communities in New Orleans, Louisiana. It took on different styles as musicians traveled the country. Some styles of jazz allow all the musicians to make up or improvise their own notes.

In other styles, just one singer improvises. Everyone else plays the melody.

SOUTHERN FOOD

Creole and Cajun cooking are famous in the South. These cooking styles blend the traditions of people who came to the region at different times. Creole cooking comes from people who came to New Orleans from the Caribbean Islands and Africa. Creole people are of mixed French or Spanish and African descent. One popular Creole dish is a seafood stew called gumbo.

QUEEN OF CREOLE CUISINE

Since the 1940s, Dooky Chase's Restaurant in New Orleans has been famous for its Creole food. The restaurant was also a meeting place for people involved in the civil rights movement. At a time when segregation laws were still enforced, people of all races ate together at Dooky Chase. Chef Leah Chase owns the restaurant. She has fed many famous customers, including presidents George W. Bush and Barack Obama. Chase is often called the "Queen of Creole Cuisine."

Spicy Cajun food is inspired by Cajun traditions. The Cajun people, also called Acadians, can trace their roots back to French settlers in Canada. One common Cajun dish is crawfish étouffée. A crawfish is similar to a small lobster.

SOUTHERN CELEBRATIONS

Thousands of people attend special events in the South each year. One popular southern event is the Daytona 500 stock car race in Florida. The race is 500 miles (805 km) long.

The most famous southern event may be Mardi Gras. It takes place each year in New Orleans. Mardi Gras is a festival that celebrates the city's French heritage. People wear costumes. They dance in the streets and throw colorful beads to each other.

The people who live in the South continue to shape southern culture. Each year, visitors from around the world travel to the region. The South offers beautiful scenery, a rich history, and many other attractions.

FURTHER EVIDENCE

Chapter Six discusses how immigrants in the South influenced its food and culture. What was one of the main points of this chapter? What key evidence supports this point? Read the article at the website below. It describes the origins of the festival Mardi Gras. Does the information on the website support one of the main points of the chapter? Or does it offer a new piece of evidence?

MARDI GRAS HISTORY
abdocorelibrary.com/exploring-south

FAST FACTS

- Total Area: 566,433 square miles (1.5 million sq km)

- Population: Approximately 82 million people

- Largest City: Jacksonville, Florida

- Largest State by Population: Florida

- Smallest State by Population: West Virginia

- Largest State by Land Size: Florida

- Smallest State by Land Size: West Virginia

- Highest Point: Mount Mitchell in North Carolina, 6,684 feet (2,036 m) above sea level

- Lowest Point: New Orleans, Louisiana, eight feet (2 m) below sea level

- Presidents: 12 US presidents came from southern states.

- Soft Drinks: Many popular sodas, including Coca Cola and Pepsi Cola, were invented in the South.

- Coastline: The South has more than 28,000 miles (45,000 km) of coastline.

- Theme Parks: Each day, nearly 53,000 people visit Walt Disney World's Magic Kingdom in Orlando, Florida. It is the most popular theme park in the United States.

STOP AND
THINK

Say What?

Studying the southern region of the United States can mean learning a lot of new words. Find five words in this book that you've never heard before. Use a dictionary to find out what they mean. Then write the meanings in your own words. Use each word in a new sentence.

Surprise Me

Chapter Two discusses the way US officials treated Native Americans living in the South. What two or three facts about this situation did you find the most surprising? Write a few sentences about each fact. Why did you find each fact surprising?

You Are There

This book covers the history, landmarks, and culture of the South. Imagine that you are planning a trip to the South. Write a journal entry about your trip. Which places would you most like to visit? What additional information would you like to learn about those areas?

Dig Deeper

After reading this book, what questions do you still have about the southern region of the United States? With an adult's help, find a few reliable sources that can help you answer your questions. Write a paragraph about what you learned.

GLOSSARY

aerospace
a technology industry that is involved in flight and space research

bayou
a swampy creek or river area

biofuel
a type of fuel made from living matter, such as plants

drone
a ship or aircraft that is steered and guided by remote control

ecosystem
all living and nonliving things in a particular environment

mangrove tree
a small tree with exposed roots that grows in tidal areas

segregation
the legal term for separating people, usually by race

sinkhole
a hole in the ground caused by water or collapse of the surface

subtropical
relating to a region near a tropical zone, with a warm and often humid climate

ONLINE
RESOURCES

To learn more about the southern region of the United States, visit our free resource websites below.

Visit **abdocorelibrary.com** for free Common Core resources for teachers and students, including vetted activities, multimedia, and booklinks, for deeper subject comprehension.

Visit **abdobooklinks.com** for free additional online weblinks for further learning. These links are routinely monitored and updated to provide the most current information available.

LEARN
MORE

Spalding, Maddie. *Everglades National Park*. Minneapolis, MN: Abdo Publishing, 2017.

Winter, Max. *The Civil Rights Movement*. Minneapolis, MN: Abdo Publishing, 2015.

INDEX

About the Author

Rebecca Stanborough has written several books for young readers. She lives and writes deep in the South, surrounded by ghostly live oak trees, giant blue herons, and even an occasional alligator.